Changing with the Times

Mutation, Variation and Adaptation Encyclopedia Kids Books Grade 7 Children's Biology Books

First Edition, 2020

Published in the United States by Speedy Publishing LLC, 40 E Main Street, Newark, Delaware 19711 USA.

Baby Professor Books are available at special discounts when purchased in bulk for industrial and sales-promotional use. For details contact our Special Sales Team at Speedy Publishing LLC, 40 E Main Street, Newark, Delaware 19711 USA. Telephone (888) 248-4521 Fax: (210) 519-4043. www.speedybookstore.com

10 9 8 7 6 * 5 4 3 2 1

Print Edition: 9781541949584
Digital Edition: 9781541951389

See the world in pictures. Build your knowledge in style.
www.speedypublishing.com

TABLE OF CONTENTS

Our world is an ever-changing place. The landforms change because of earthquakes, flooding, erosion, and fire. Oceans and seas change because of pollution, climate change, and violent storms. Did you know that the plants and the animals of the planet are also constantly changing? You may have heard terms such as evolution and natural selection before and wondered how that causes plants and animals to change over time. In this book, we will explore that question and learn the meanings of mutation, variation, and adaptation. Let's get started.

Chameleon adapted to his green scenery

WHY DO PLANTS AND ANIMALS CHANGE?

This is an important question. If an animal or plant is ideally developed to thrive in its native habitat, why would it ever need to change? In many cases, the environment in which the plant or animal lives changes over time, therefore the living organism must also change to adjust to its new environment.

Two different habitats where different animals and plants thrive.

Other changes happen by accident and on an individual basis. One animal, for example, can have an error occur in its genetic sequencing, causing it to have a different trait than others of its species. Its offspring may inherit that trait and pass it on to their own offspring.

An animals genetic code may be different than that of its species resulting in a difference in traits.

WHAT ARE MUTATIONS?

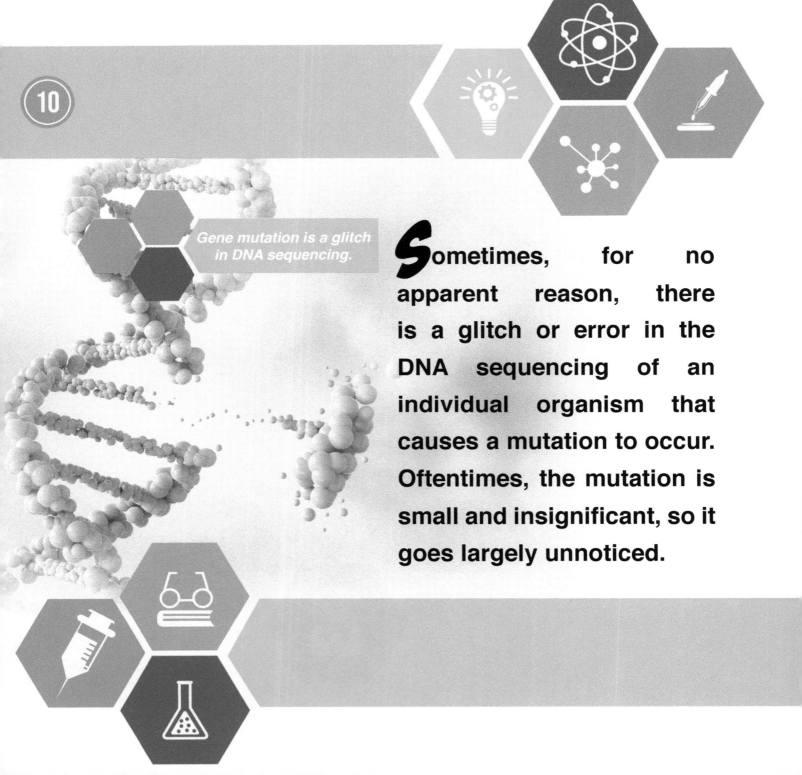

10

Gene mutation is a glitch in DNA sequencing.

Sometimes, for no apparent reason, there is a glitch or error in the DNA sequencing of an individual organism that causes a mutation to occur. Oftentimes, the mutation is small and insignificant, so it goes largely unnoticed.

But other times, the mutation is outwardly noticeable. It may drastically alter the life of the animal, for the better or for the worse.

Tree frog with one eye

For example, a genetic[1] mutation in a bird may cause it to be born with a misshapen beak. The mutant beak could inhibit the bird from properly eating, leading to malnutrition and death. Or, the mutant beak could be beneficial for cracking open specific seeds or clam shells, helping the bird to live a robust and healthy life.

1 Genetic – Relating to genes and DNA.

A chick with a deformed beak

Since the mutation is permanently encoded into the animal's DNA, it can be inherited by its offspring. In this manner, the mutation can spread throughout the population. But the mutation begins with just one organism, therefore it takes many generations before it is widespread.

Long-tailed Shrike with a beak deformity

EXAMPLES OF MUTATIONS

A genetic mutation can be both harmful and advantageous. Some mutations of DNA can lead to congenital diseases. In humans, cystic fibrosis, sickle cell anemia, and muscular dystrophy are all caused by mutations in the DNA of a person.

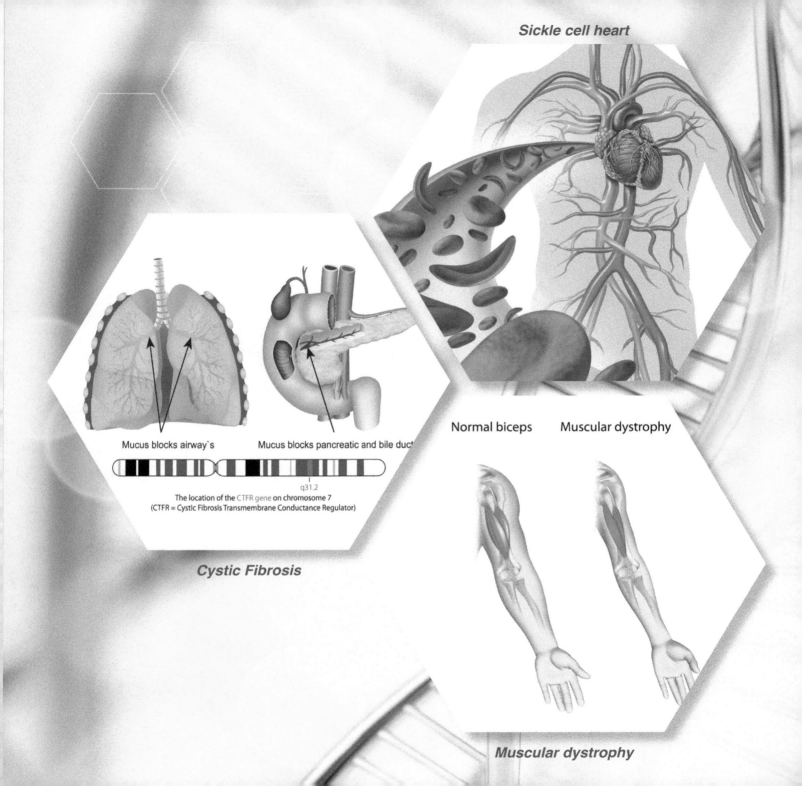

Sickle cell heart

Normal biceps   Muscular dystrophy

Mucus blocks airway`s   Mucus blocks pancreatic and bile duct

q31.2

The location of the CTFR gene on chromosome 7
(CTFR = Cystic Fibrosis Transmembrane Conductance Regulator)

Cystic Fibrosis

Muscular dystrophy

A genetic mutation in animals may alter the color of the individual animal.

Rare polka-dotted zebra

Occasionally, commercial fishermen find a rare blue lobster and hunters report seeing deer with patches of all white fur. These are the results of genetic mutations.

Blue lobster

WHAT ARE VARIATIONS?

While an adaptation is a change that happens as a result of outside changes, a variation is a difference that has always existed within a population of animals or plants.

A horse with distinctive tiger eye

This is a genetic or developmental anomaly of a daisy

Variations can show up as visible or measurable traits, like appearance, coloring, behavior, and intelligence. They can also be unseen traits, such as metabolism and internal functions.

Four horn goat with genetic anomalies

The variations manifest because of genetic patterns or anomalies in the chromosomes. Unlike adaptations, variations are not linked to heredity and do not have a major impact on evolution.

EXAMPLES OF VARIATIONS

In the plant world, we see variations in the leaf shapes and flower colors on the same type of plants. A rose, for example, can be red, yellow, white, or pink.

Assorted colors of the rose flower

In humans, people can have different blood types, hair color, eye color, and unique features, such as freckles, moles, or dimples.

Different people with different traits

All of the different combinations of variables are locked in the individual plant, animal, or person's genetic code and appear as a happenstance of birth.

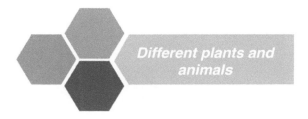

Different plants and animals

WHAT ARE ADAPTATIONS?

In general, an adaptation in a living organism is a change or adjustment that all or most of its species undergoes so that it can thrive in its native habitat.

Native habitat of the fish

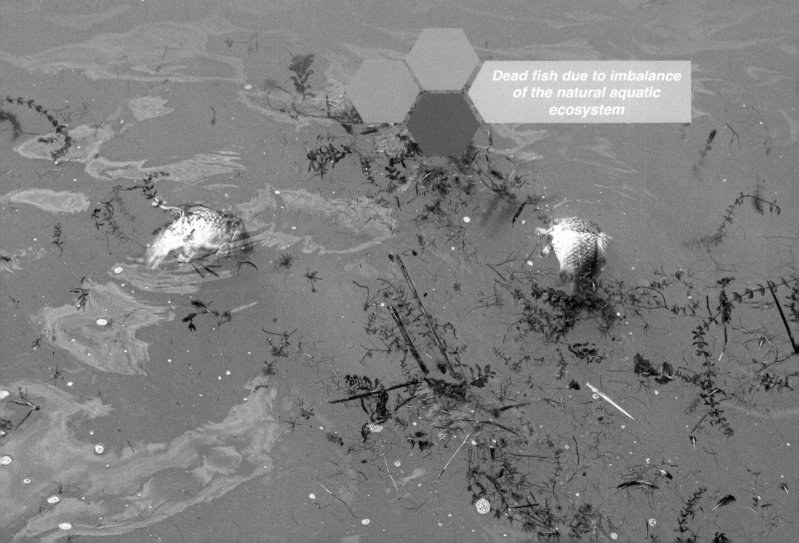

If there is a change in the habitat where the plant or animal lives, that change could impact the growth, reproduction, and even survival of the species.

Dead fish due to imbalance of the natural aquatic ecosystem

If the area gets less rainfall than normal or a common food source dies out, a species of animals must adapt to the situation to increase its survival rates.

Ground drought due to less rainfall.

EXAMPLES OF ADAPTATIONS

Some animals adapt to better suit their environment by developing a way to blend in with their surroundings. Some insects, like katydids, have adapted to look like leaves, for example, and other animals, like zebras, have a patterned coat to camouflage them in tall grass.

Zebras have a patterned coat to blend with the tall grass.

Other living organisms have adapted their eating habits to accommodate the available food sources. The Venus flytrap, for instance, makes its home in such nutrient poor soil that it has adapted a way of capturing and eating insects in order to get the nutrients it was missing from its environment.

Venus fly trap

WHAT IS EVOLUTION?

When the traits and characteristics that are hereditary, or can be passed down from parent to offspring, begin to change it means that, from one generation to the next, there are slow and subtle changes.

Female cheetah with cubs

It takes time for the changes to spread through the entire population. It also takes time for ineffective evolutionary traits to die out in favor of effective ones. The process is very slow. It can take hundreds of thousands of years for the change to become commonplace.

Sex-linked Dominant Hereditary Trait

SEX-LINKED DOMINANT

Father with Abnormal Gene on **X** Sex Chromosome

Mother with Normal **X** Sex Chromosomes

PARENTS: XY   XX

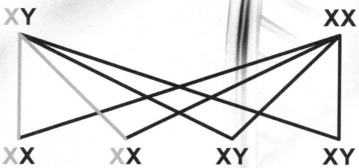

OFFSPRING: XX   XX   XY   XY

Female offsprings receive abnormal gene.
Male offsprings do not receive abnormal gene.

A CONTROVERSIAL THEORY

Noted naturalist Charles Darwin was one of the early proponents of the theory that plants and animals evolve to suit their environment.

Charles Darwin

He made this theory after observing finches in the Galapagos Islands off the coast of South America. The birds on the various islands, he observed, had different shaped beaks that were ideal for cracking open the unique seeds on their own island.

The Galapagos
Islands, Ecuador

He realized that the birds have changed over time to fit their environment. At the time, Darwin's ideas were controversial[2] because they ran counter to biblical teachings, but eventually, his theory became accepted as scientific fact.

2 Controversial – Debatable or arguable.

Reptile and birds of Galapagos islands

EXAMPLES OF EVOLUTIONARY CHANGE

Although it is a slow process, scientists have been able to record numerous cases of evolutionary changes in a variety of animals and plants. In one case, a reptile called the cane toad was introduced into Australia.

Cane toad

Cane toads changed to adapt to their new home in Australia.

An invasive species, the toads changed to adapt to their new home. Their hind legs became longer and stronger and the overall body of the toad was stronger and hardier.

A native of the United States, the rat snake can be found in several different colors, depending on whether it is found in the desert regions or the forests and grasslands. There are also insects that have adapted to be immune to pesticides.

Texas rat snake

Green rat snake

Black Rat Snake

Wild red rat snake

WHAT IS NATURAL SELECTION?

*S*ome of the new traits or characteristics are a benefit to the animal species and some are not. Natural selection happens when the more advantageous traits help the living organism to live and thrive while the organisms with inferior traits die out. Over time, more of the organisms with the better traits reproduce and spread those traits to the subsequent generations.

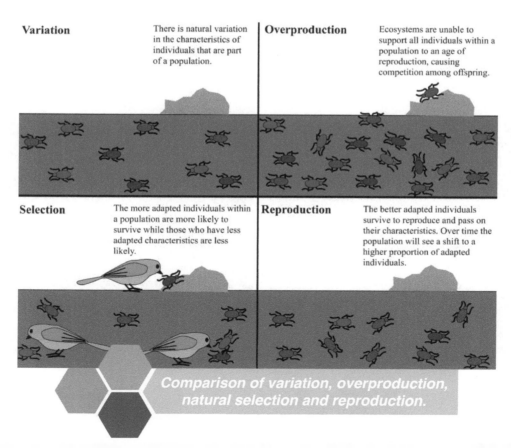

Variation — There is natural variation in the characteristics of individuals that are part of a population.

Overproduction — Ecosystems are unable to support all individuals within a population to an age of reproduction, causing competition among offspring.

Selection — The more adapted individuals within a population are more likely to survive while those who have less adapted characteristics are less likely.

Reproduction — The better adapted individuals survive to reproduce and pass on their characteristics. Over time the population will see a shift to a higher proportion of adapted individuals.

Comparison of variation, overproduction, natural selection and reproduction.

These traits become so common in that species that nearly all of the population has it. In this manner, the advantageous trait has evolved naturally to become a dominant characteristic.

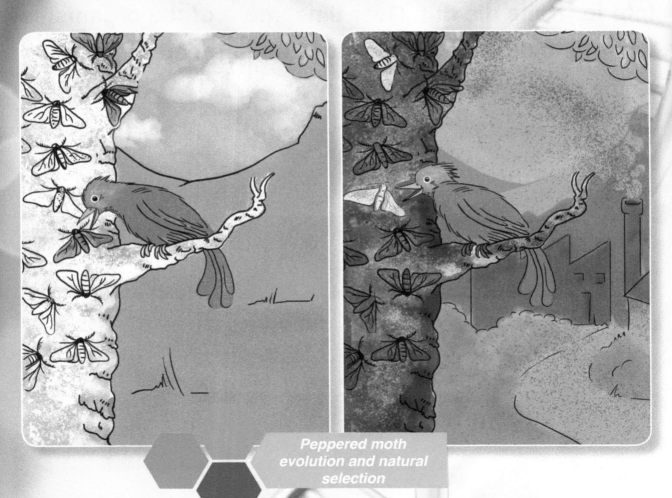

Peppered moth evolution and natural selection

EXAMPLES OF NATURAL SELECTION

Some of the most unique features in some animals may be the product of natural selection. Take the giraffe, for example. Its long neck is a result of natural selection. Animals with longer necks could reach the leaves at the top of the trees – an advantageous trait – so over thousands of years, the neck of the giraffe got longer and longer.

Giraffe eating from the tree

Likewise, penguins changed to fit their Antarctic habitat. The ability to fly was no longer vital to survival, but the ability to swim was.

Penguins leaping into the ocean

The penguins that were the strongest swimmers thrived until all penguins lost their flight and gained skills in swimming.

Penguins swimming underwater

WHAT IS SELECTIVE BREEDING?

Breeder of dogs with her pets

In the natural world, mutations, variations, and adaptations occur naturally, but humans have been doing an artificial form of natural selection for hundreds of years. Take, for example, the hobby of dog breeding.

A good, reputable dog breeder aims to produce top quality puppies with the ideal traits and characteristics that are ideal for its breed.

A breeder with her top quality dogs

They do this by intentionally breeding a dog with the sought-after trait with another with similar traits.

Breed of dachshund puppies

Humans also do selective breeding with **livestock**[3] animals, such as cattle, hogs, sheep, and horses.

3 Livestock – Animals domesticated for farm use.

Selective breeding is also done on livestock like cows and sheep.

SUMMARY

All living things on Earth are in constant change. Species adapt to the changing environment or develop traits[4] that help them thrive. Traits that are helpful to the species eventually spread through the whole population. Even though many people were leery of Charles Darwin's theory of evolution, in truth, humans had been employing selective breeding techniques in livestock animals for hundreds of years in attempts to breed superior animals.

4 Trait – A characteristic or quality.

Now that you have learned about mutations, variations, and adaptations, you should read more about genetics and DNA to help you better understand heredity and evolution.

Visit

www.speedypublishing.com

to download Free Baby Professor eBooks

and view our catalog of new and exciting

Children's Books

Lightning Source UK Ltd.
Milton Keynes UK
UKHW050749050121
376449UK00002B/38

9 781541 980310